A Mississippi Morning on Bluebird Hill

Chickens, Chickens and More Chickens

Printed in the United States of America.

ISBN SOFT COVER: 978-1-59571-520-3
ISBN HARD COVER: 978-1-59571-524-1

LIBRARY OF CONGRESS NUMBER: 2010924832

Designed and published by

Word Association Publishers
205 Fifth Avenue
Tarentum, Pennsylvania 15084

Photographs and stories by Billie Remson
Sunrise on Bluebird Hill by God

www.wordassociation.com
1 800 827 7903

OTHER BOOKS BY BILLIE REMSON

A Mississippi Spring On Bluebird Hill

A Mississippi Summer On Bluebird Hill

Katrina and the Unforgettable Mississippi Autumn On Bluebird Hill

A Mississippi Winter On Bluebird Hill

A Mississippi Morning on Bluebird Hill

Chickens, Chickens and More Chickens

BILLIE REMSON

"Mama B"

Table of Contents

How it All Began 1

Bo and the Opossum 7

Chickens, Chickens, and More Chickens 23

The Big Fat White Chicken 41

Mama B's Chicken Gumbo 58

The Love of a Mother Hen 63

A Surprise in the Chicken House 67

The Chickens Escape 87

Miss Katie and the Wooden Egg 97

Mr. and Mrs. Whitehead 103

From Stray Dog to Calendar Girl in Nine Months 113

BEAUREGARD IN HIS FULL BEAUTY

In Memory of Bo

BEAUREGARD "BO"
REMSON'S PRIDE,
A SHETLAND SHEEPDOG

March 1, 1998 - December 13, 2007

My love for Bo only deepens as I write about Bluebird Hill and remember what a fun and energetic companion he was to Mama B, Papa Doc, Snow the cat, and all the animals of Bluebird Hill. Readers who have loved Bo and followed him in the Bluebird Hill series of books will again share his adventures. To those of you who are newcomers to our little Mississippi farm family, I am thrilled to introduce you to my beloved Bo.

BILLIE REMSON

So Long to Bo, Mississippi's Beloved Sheltie

"He allowed others to pet him endlessly and watch him perform majestically, waving his beautiful white-tipped tail at book signings, school readings, and when company came to call. Although Bo's tail has wagged for the last time, his love and friendship live in our hearts. Bo brought happiness, joy, freedom to frolic, a little slice of heaven on earth, and good fortune to everyone who knew him."

JO MCDIVITT — Owner and Editor of *Today's Mississippi Woman* magazine.

Dedication

IN HONOR OF OUR NEW ADDITION,

GINNY JO, ADOPTED FEBRUARY 22, 2008

May 21, 1989

How it All Began

Doctor Marcel Remson, a dentist from Houma, Louisiana, and Miss Billie, a lady from Jackson, Mississippi, met on a cruise ship just two hours after he boarded the ship in Puerto Rico. They were seated at the same table for dinner and, as happens, struck up a conversation. Soon they learned that both had lost their spouses during the past year after thirty years of marriage. As the evening went on, they found they had even more in common and that they enjoyed each other's company. The two courted throughout the cruise under the watchful eyes of Billie's traveling companions, her two daughters. The courtship turned into a beautiful relationship and the happy couple married fifteen months after they met. Billie then moved from Jackson, Mississippi, to live with her new husband in Houma, Louisiana, fifty-five miles southwest of New Orleans.

During this time of change in their lives, their first grandchild was born and Billie and Marcel became Mama B and Papa Doc. For Mama B, it was the geography and culture of southern Louisiana that presented a far greater challenge than the newness of her marriage or the pleasures of a grandchild. Shrimp boats going up and down the

bayous just outside their Houma windows were a far cry from the quiet rivers and streams of Mama B's Mississippi home. And it took a while for Mama B to become accustomed to Louisiana's fields of sugar cane and marshland inhabited by alligators, when she was used to Mississippi's fields of snow-white cotton and rolling hills covered with pine trees. In time, however, Mama B came to enjoy her new life, new friends, and the exotic and wonderful food of bayou country. Before long, Mama B's favorite dish of Mississippi chicken 'n dumplings gave way to Louisiana's famous seafood gumbo. She even learned the proper language for giving directions in bayou country. It's *up* the bayou, *down* the bayou, and *across* the bayou. Even so, Mama B never forgot her small-town farm roots in Mississippi. Coincidentally, Papa Doc, who had grown up in the city of New Orleans, had a lifelong dream of owning a parcel of land large enough to drive around on

She even learned the proper language for giving directions in bayou country. It's *up* the bayou, *down* the bayou, and *across* the bayou.

The Remson farmhouse on Bluebird Hill

and enjoy the wildlife. That was just fine with Mama B because she missed the rural life she had cherished as a young girl. Finally, after eight years in Louisiana, Mama B and Papa Doc became the proud owners of two hundred acres of land in south central Mississippi.

The first thing they built on the land was a cozy farmhouse. Next came a large pond for fish and the planting of one hundred fifty acres of pine trees. Once the farm was up and running, Mama B and Papa Doc began to notice the many bluebirds who clearly considered this farm home. It became obvious to both of them that they had built their cozy little farmhouse on land that they just had to name Bluebird Hill.

Papa Doc's dream of a farm had finally come true. Mama B was also thrilled except that, in her opinion, every farm has to have a dog. Bo, a Shetland Sheepdog puppy, was a had-to-have for Mama B, and of course Papa Doc indulged her wish. Next, Rufus, a rooster, and several Bantam hens moved into the new chicken house. The chickens were fascinating to Mama B's watchful eyes and soon she was sending e-mails to family and friends about her new life on the farm. Mama B had no idea the hobby of photographing and writing about her chicken family would soon change her life forever.

Marcel, Billie, and Goldie at home on Bluebird Hill

Mama B had no idea the hobby of photographing and writing about her chicken family would soon change her life forever.

One day Rufus the rooster and his little hen friends provided the perfect shot for Mama B's new camera. The picture of the little Bantam chickens was good enough to be painted by an artist they knew who specializes in watercolor. When Mama B told the watercolorist about the popularity of the e-mails she was writing and how everyone wanted to know more and more about the farm and the adventures she and Papa Doc were having, the artist asked if she had considered writing a book about Bluebird Hill. But Mama B just didn't know. She was sixty-two years old and she did not know about starting something so new and ambitious that late in life. But the artist had planted a seed, a seed that germinated and grew. Soon, what started with a chicken, a picture, and a rambunctious puppy became a series of books about the inhabitants of Bluebird Hill and life on a farm just for the fun of it.

You never know when a new road will open in your life and where it will take you. No matter what age you are, have faith as you travel it and see where it leads. I did, and I love it. I'm seventy now and this is my fifth book. I consider myself a visual writer. I try to put into words exactly what I see, for others to enjoy.

BILLIE REMSON

"If you have faith no bigger even than a mustard seed, nothing will prove impossible to you."

Matthew 17:20

Bo

Bo and the Opossum

The grass is wet with dew that has fallen during the night on Bluebird Hill. Papa Doc cannot mow with the tractor until the grass dries. He is not a happy farmer, because mowing the grass with the tractor is his favorite chore on the farm. This will possibly be the last mowing for the summer as the cool nights of autumn have arrived on Bluebird Hill.

A Bluebird Hill rooster announcing the dawn

Rufus, Lili, Spec, and all the other roosters are crowing, announcing it's time to get up and get moving. (Before we go on, you need to know that Lili's name is pronounced Lilly but spelled Lili because he and another biddy were hatched between two hurricanes. The storms were named Lili and Isidore and Mama B thought those names appropriate for her new babies—both of whom turned out to be roosters.)

Hearing the sounds from the chicken yard reminds Mama B that the chickens are waiting to be fed. In addition, the songbirds are calling her attention to the birdfeeders reminding her that a new supply of sunflower seeds is needed. The birdbath must be scrubbed and filled with water. Mama B looks up as the ruby-throated hummingbirds circle their feeders waiting for a refill. They are fueling their bodies, preparing for a long flight south before winter. They usually leave Bluebird Hill in the middle of October. These are all small jobs that require attention, but they are not work for Mama B because she enjoys doing them just as much as Papa Doc enjoys driving the tractor. She does not fuss—she is happy on Bluebird Hill. There, she and Papa Doc spend most of their time outside, enjoying the beautiful days with Bo close by.

Once the sun dries the grass, Papa Doc begins mowing and this sets off the bluebirds scouting for food. The mower is stirring up the insects and the bluebirds are ready for them. They are meat eaters and their diet is mainly insects. The bluebirds are finding plenty of crickets, grasshoppers, and other insects for their breakfast. Papa Doc is certainly their friend today.

Mama B, Papa Doc, and Bo spend much of their time observing and enjoying the animals. Since Bo is a working dog, he enjoys a good rabbit chase on his morning walk outside the yard fence. He knows Mama B does not like him to chase the rabbits close to the farmhouse because she thinks the rabbits who live inside her yard fence are pets same as Bo and the chickens. Bo stands very still and watches a rabbit for a few minutes and when it is more than he can stand, off he goes as fast as his legs will carry him, on a great chase, until the rabbit dives into the briars for protection.

Mama B thinks this rabbit enjoys Bo chasing him.

Mama B thinks the rabbits enjoy the action as much as Bo since there is always one waiting for Bo in the same spot every morning.

When they finish their walk and arrive back at the farmhouse, Mama B stops on the porch and puts on her chicken yard shoes and bonnet. Bo stands very still and waits for her next move toward the chicken house. One step off the porch and it is a short distance to the barn. The chickens are waiting to be fed, and judging by the noise coming from the chicken house, there will be fresh eggs to gather for a good country breakfast. (For those not familiar with chickens, there is a big commotion in the chicken house when a chicken lays an egg. The lady of the hour gets off the warm, wet egg, perches on the wood frame of the nest, and cackles for the entire world to hear of her accomplishment. Most of her chicken friends chime in by squawking, crowing, or making whatever noise they can to celebrate the newly laid egg. Most eggs are laid early in the morning, making the chicken house a noisy place.)

Inside the barn where the chicken feed is stored, Mama B sees a mouse eating some corn that has spilled onto the floor. Bo runs after the mouse while Mama B fills her feed bucket. Soon Bo is sniffing in the corner of the barn where the mouse has escaped through a little hole.

Mama B feeding her chickens

After a short walk to the chicken house Mama B feeds the chickens and gathers the eggs, putting them in her feed bucket. Bo has made it to the chicken yard and is playing a game with the chickens by running up to the fence, barking, and running away. It is fun for him, but the chickens are busy eating and are not paying Bo any attention.

When Mama B counts her chickens, she realizes a Bantam hen is missing. She searches frantically but the little Bantam is not in the chicken house or in the chicken yard. She is gone. There is not a feather left. Mama B is heartsick as she retraces her steps looking for

> When Mama B counts her chickens, she realizes a Bantam hen is missing.

evidence that might tell her what happened to her dear little hen. But she finds nothing and goes through the wooden gate to continue her search. Bo, who has been anxiously waiting outside the chicken yard, leads the way around the side of the chicken yard to the back of the chicken house. Being a Shetland Sheepdog, Bo is alert to any change and quickly spots the small hole and pile of dirt.

Since the floor of the chicken house is dirt, an animal can dig a hole outside, go under the wall, and come up on the inside of the chicken house. The pile of dirt shows Mama B that an animal was trying to do just that but failed. The dirt was not there the day before. The animal must have been digging during the night, but there has been no rain for several days and the dirt is dry and too hard to dig. The animal had to find another way to get in.

Bo picks up the scent of the animal and with his nose to the ground and his white-tipped tail wagging high in the air, he leads Mama B around the chicken yard fence where he abruptly loses the scent.

The chicken yard is enclosed with a wire fence and wire roof to

View of the chicken yard

keep out hawks, owls, and other animals that will harm the chickens. While inspecting the wire fence and wire roof to find the way the animal got in, Mama B sees a loose wire on top of the chicken yard fence where the wire joins the chicken house. She also notices gray fur on the sharp edges of the wire. This tells her an animal climbed the wire fence and got in through the top of the chicken yard fence where the wire joins the chicken house.

Mama B is upset over the loss of the little Bantam hen and knows the repair to the fence has to be made immediately. This is a busy time of the year for Papa Doc and she does not want to bother him with mending the fence. She can handle this chore herself to help keep her precious chickens safe.

Walking hurriedly into the barn, Mama B gets an eight-foot ladder, a pocket full of staples, and a hammer. She is ready, willing, and able to handle this job. Once she's up on the ladder, she hammers the staples across the wire, attaching it securely to the chicken house. Even though she smashes her finger with the hammer a few times, Mama B never gives up until she is satisfied that her chickens are protected from the intruder.

It must have been a big opossum or raccoon that made its way into the chicken yard. Whatever that animal was, thinks Mama B as she takes her ladder and tools back to the barn, he will not get in our chicken house again.

After putting the ladder and tools away, Mama B returns to the chicken house for the bucket of eggs. On the way to the house, she counts the eggs and there is an even dozen. "Looks like the laying mash is paying off," Mama B tells Bo.

There have been very few eggs due to molting of the chickens in early autumn. The hens use their energy to produce feathers they lose during molting. They need their feathers to protect them during the cold winter ahead, and the process of laying eggs almost stops during this time. "It's good they are laying again. That means Papa Doc and I will have fresh eggs with our breakfast." Mama B likes talking to Bo when Papa Doc is not around for her to talk to. Bo's ears are always eager to listen. Bo loves her as much as she loves him.

Three nights later as the cuckoo clock announces ten-thirty, Papa Doc is in the tub taking a long soaking bath. Mama B has already taken her bath, is in her pajamas, and is ready to go to bed. But before she can do that she remembers that Bo has been a busy dog running and playing in the yard during the afternoon and has been drinking a lot of water. With this in mind Mama B decides it would be a good idea to take Bo outside for one last tinkle. As Mama B puts on her blue robe and gets the flashlight, Bo knows by her action that it is time to go outside and he stands patiently at the door waiting.

> Mama B never gives up until she is satisfied that her chickens are protected from the intruder.

A damp mist is falling and a cool breeze is blowing. Mama B, however, is going out anyway because she does not want Bo to go outside alone at night. She worries about the packs of coyotes that roam the woods. Even though he is not afraid of anything, Mama B is as protective of Bo as he is of her.

Bo stays close by Mama B until they reach the corner of the picket fence that encloses the flower garden. Suddenly he takes off to the far side of the flower garden fence, running as fast as his four legs can carry him. He stays for a few minutes and runs back to Mama B. Again and again, Bo runs back and forth from where Mama B is standing near the other side of the picket fence. Each time, he stops in front of Mama B and looks up at her as if to say please come with me—hurry! Mama B can see that Bo is trying to tell her something. Since Bo is a Shetland Sheepdog, he is normally loud and vocal when he wants to make a statement. But on this night he is intense, anxious, and strangely quiet as he does his best to relay a message to Mama B.

With the flashlight shining, Mama B walks the short distance to the far side of the picket fence. Bo is standing very still. He is looking down at the ground. Much to Mama B's surprise there is a big opossum playing dead by the picket fence. The opossum's mouth is wide open and his tongue is hanging out. Mama B knows that when frightened and unable to get away, an opossum will fall into a shock-like state—playing possum. An opossum will play possum until the danger is over and then crawl off when no one is watching. (In case you were wondering, some people call them possums and some call them opossums and, according to *Webster's,* both are correct.)

Mama B remembers what happened at the chicken house a few nights back. Could this be the animal that got her little Bantam hen?

Bo shows Mama B the "dead" opossum.

His fur is gray and the fur on the wire was gray. With this thought Mama B runs to the front door, opens it quickly, and yells, "Papa Doc, get out of the tub! There is a big opossum at the edge of the flower garden and you need to do something with him before he gets in the chicken house."

Papa Doc is not very happy with Mama B for disturbing his bath because of an opossum. He likes to take long hot baths and has been known to take a nap in the tub. Although Papa Doc wants to stay in the warm, soothing water, he knows that he better do as Mama B is asking and take care of that opossum. If that opossum gets in the chicken house again, the furry intruder may eat more than one chicken.

Papa Doc puts on his pajamas, a robe, and his boots and hurries to the barn in the damp, dark night to get a chicken pen. When he returns with the pen, he picks the opossum up by the tail and locks him in the pen. "Tomorrow, I will relocate that opossum, Mama B," he says, half asleep, and walks back into the house muttering to himself. Papa Doc does not like to relocate animals from Bluebird Hill but when intruders get into the chicken house and steal chickens, it upsets Mama B and when Mama B is upset over the loss of her chickens, Papa Doc is upset.

Mama B and Bo finally continue the walk they started earlier on down Rabbit Run Road so that Bo can tinkle. Mama B is pleased she does not have to worry about the opossum getting back into the chicken house. With the work she did mending the wire on the chicken yard roof and the opossum now trapped she feels fairly certain that her chickens are safe.

When Mama B and Bo return to the house after their delayed walk, it is bedtime at last. Papa Doc and Mama B climb into bed, Bo curls up on the floor at the foot of the bed, and they all go to sleep.

It is early in the morning when they awaken to the sound of Rufus's crow and a lot of chicken chatter coming from the hen house. Perhaps the chickens are celebrating the departure of the opossum. Bo waits patiently for Mama B to finish her coffee before going to the door and barking to go outside. He is surely remembering last night's adventure, thinking of the opossum and, for that matter, so is Mama B. When she opens the door and they go outside together, Bo runs around the corner of the picket fence to the other side of the flower garden with Mama B close behind him. Both are in a hurry because Papa Doc is on his way to get the truck and pick up the opossum to relocate him. Mama B is anxious to see if the opossum is as large as

He is proud because he has succeeded with the meanest of all possum tricks on Mama B, Papa Doc, and Bo.

he seemed the night before.

Papa Doc is just getting out of the truck when Mama B and Bo reach the pen and all three are stunned by what they find. There is no opossum anywhere. That cunning creature pulled the old opossum stunt and played possum until everyone went inside for the night. Then the clever thing discovered a way to open the door of the chicken pen and crawl off. Most likely, that crafty old boy is sitting in the top of a persimmon tree somewhere on the farm with his big grin, showing all fifty teeth. He is proud because he has succeeded with the meanest of all possum tricks on Mama B, Papa Doc, and Bo. "That's the way opossums do," Mama B tells Papa Doc as Bo looks up at her with his ears pointed and big brown eyes shining. Papa Doc puts the chicken pen in the back of the truck and returns it to the barn. He washes it out and repairs the door where the opossum chewed around the lock. They'll all have to stay on the alert for that old opossum and make sure he doesn't go after any more of their chickens.

It is such a pretty morning that Mama B joins Bo for his walk down Rabbit Run Road. Bo sees the little rabbit that Mama B likes to watch from her kitchen window as he plays in the yard. The rabbit is nibbling grass and looks up and sees Bo. Bo, in turn, looks up at Mama B as if to say, Do you mind if I chase that rabbit? Without a nod of approval from Mama B, Bo decides to take off after the rabbit anyway. As usual, the rabbit chase stops when the rabbit enters the briar patch at the edge of the yard. Bo is getting his morning exercise and so is the rabbit, so Mama B doesn't mind. When Bo returns, they go back to the farmhouse and Bo lies down on the floor and closes his eyes. As he sleeps, you can tell that Bo is probably dreaming about the return visit of the opossum. Everyone knows it's just a matter of time. Soon Bo's legs begin moving in his sleep. His eyes are twitching. Does he see the big opossum? Suddenly Bo awakens, and stands quickly. His ears straighten and his eyes are wide open. He looks as if he is going to take off running.

Bo looks over at Mama B, who is standing near the kitchen stove, and realizes he has been dreaming. He walks over to the front door, lies down, and looks out. Perhaps he is thinking as he looks through the glass door to the yard outside—*next time, next time, I will get him! Another day, another time, and he is mine!*

SnowBall (a Silkie)

Chickens, Chickens, and More Chickens

W*e do not need any more chickens on Bluebird Hill. We do not need any more chickens on Bluebird Hill. We do not need any more chickens on Bluebird Hill!* Mama B tells herself again and again as she walks in the door of Tylertown Farm Supply to buy chicken feed. Papa Doc has said these exact words many times and she's fairly certain that repeating them as she enters the store will strengthen her resolve. But suddenly she hears chirping and, looking toward the sound, she sees baby chicks. The chicks, sometimes called biddies, are eating and running around in what looks like a playpen but is really just a square area walled in by large sacks of grain.

Springtime in the South is biddie-hatching time and Mama B cannot keep her eyes off the tiny chicks in the playpen. Papa Doc's words of *chickens, chickens, and more chickens, we do not need any more chickens on Bluebird Hill* are still going through Mama B's mind. But these biddies are one week old and they are the prettiest biddies she has ever seen. The white fuzz on the tiptop of their tiny heads looks

Mama B's favorite shopping spot.

like little white pompoms. The remainder of their tiny bodies is covered in dark fuzz.

"What breed are they?" asks Mama B, already pretty certain that she's not going to be able to resist the chicks—even though she knows that if Papa Doc was with her, she would not be buying any more chickens for Bluebird Hill.

"Straight run, White Crested Black Polish, shipped in from Wisconsin," the lady behind the counter replies.

"I would like two," says Mama B without a moment's hesitation.

"The ones over here, what breed are they?" Mama B wants to know.

Mama B cannot resist the soft little biddies.

"Silkies, feather footed-Bantams, all female," replies the lady.

"I have to have three of those. I want a white, a black, and a blue," says an excited Mama B.

She picks up two of the biddies and holds them in the palm of her hand. Their bodies are covered in soft silky fuzz. They are about an inch high and just adorable. Mama B is thinking they are the cutest, most unusual biddies she has ever seen. They will certainly fit in with the other chickens on Bluebird Hill. She wants a flock of assorted chickens at the farm and these biddies will give her something different from her small Bantam chickens.

"Oh yes," Mama B almost forgot to say, "I'm here to buy chicken feed. I would like a forty-pound bag of chicken scratch, forty pounds of laying mash, and twenty pounds of growing mash for my new biddies."

The chicken feed is loaded in the back of her truck. The biddies she was not supposed to buy are placed in a small box. Holding the little cardboard box in her hands, Mama B walks out of the store and places it carefully on the front seat of her white pickup truck. The five little biddies inside the cardboard box chirp, scratch, and peck all the way home to Bluebird Hill.

As Mama B arrives on Bluebird Hill she sees Papa Doc and Bo near the chicken yard. Papa Doc is enjoying this pretty day in southern Mississippi by preparing the soil to plant the spring vegetable garden. Bo is on a trail with his nose to the ground, sniffing around in the grass.

A buzzard in the sky casts a fast-moving shadow over Bo. Now Bo has to decide whether to chase the shadow of the buzzard or see if Mama B has brought him a treat. Chasing the shadow of the buzzard seems more appealing. And if Mama B brought him a treat, he can just get it later. As fast as a flash of lightning, Bo takes off running, following the shadow of the buzzard. He thinks he is the protector of the air as well as the earth on Bluebird Hill. All of it is his territory and with his bark he is telling the buzzard to stay away. He tries his best to keep the farm safe from anything he thinks will harm his Bluebird Hill family.

Mama B does not know what Papa Doc is going to say about the new biddies. She knew before she bought them that there were enough chickens on Bluebird Hill but she just could not say no to such unusual chicks. Mama B has learned that each breed of chickens has its own personality. The more the better is Mama B's philosophy even though she knows she truly does have enough chickens to care for. More chickens, more work.

Papa Doc is busy unloading the sacks of chicken feed and does not see Mama B getting the tiny box from inside the pickup truck. Bo has returned from the buzzard chase. He gets a drink of water and lies down in the grass, to cool off, when he hears the chirping of the new biddies. He is so excited he forgets about a treat. He barks and jumps up and down near Mama B, nearly knocking the biddy box out of her hands. As Mama B tries to calm Bo with a treat from her pocket, Papa Doc hears the ruckus and comes around the truck to

She replaces the newspaper several times a day because little biddies make big messes.

see what the fuss is about. When he sees Mama B holding the small box with little round holes cut out for ventilation, he knows that more biddies have come to live on Bluebird Hill.

Mama B takes a deep breath and tells him she has just purchased five of the cutest little biddies she has ever seen. Papa Doc has heard that before and shakes his head as if to say, well, you did it again. Carefully, Mama B opens the box and when Papa Doc sees the beautiful little puffs of fuzz, he can't help but agree with Mama B and in the end he is very happy that she bought the biddies. When Mama B is happy, Papa Doc is happy. And Bo is wagging his white-tipped, fluffy tail because he is happy too.

Until they get a little older, the new biddies will make their home in a large cardboard box. Mama B has put several layers of newspaper in the bottom of the box. She replaces the newspaper several times a day because little biddies make big messes. She puts their food of growing mash in a feeder inside the box. As soon as she fills their water container, the fun begins. The biddies get their feet wet by standing in the water container. Then they start pecking their food out of the feeder and the food falls on the newspaper. When they walk over the newspaper, bits of food attach to their wet feet and get tracked all over the newspaper. Then the biddies peck and scratch the newspaper and the mess continues. But it's all a part of their learning and even if they had a mother hen, she would be encouraging them to do just what they are doing.

Little biddies make big messes.

Mother hens use their instinct to teach and care for their biddies and to train them just as human mothers do. The biddies follow their mother's instructions by imitating what she is doing. She is not teaching them to make a mess. She is teaching them to care for their needs and to survive by eating. When the babies are about two days old, they start feeding lessons. They watch their mother peck a grain of food and take a drink of water and they mirror her actions. But like human toddlers, biddies get all carried away and do not understand the mess they are making by jumping back and forth on the newspaper between their water and their food. To them, it is not making a mess but rather their way of learning and having fun along the way. Mother hens are just like human mothers who understand that their little ones can't help being messy.

Although it takes a little longer, biddies that don't have their mothers with them will eventually learn the same technique that the mother hen would have taught them. They watch each other and if one takes a drink of water or eats food the others do the same thing. Sometimes Mama B helps them by putting their beaks in their water for the first time. She taps her finger on the newspaper like a mother hen does with her beak to show them how to peck the food from the newspaper.

Mama B's new babies are smart little biddies. When one biddy finds food on the newspaper and starts pecking, all the other little biddies hear the noise and come running to see what it has. When another takes a drink by putting its beak in the water and raising its head back to swallow, the others have to have a drink too. While running to the water, they jump and fly up in the air, trying to see who can out-jump the other. All of this might appear to be silly play, but the biddies are really learning all that will be necessary for them to grow up.

When the biddies finish drinking, they go back to the feeders and jump up on top of the water container. Over in the corner, one pecks at another's toes. It jumps on the back of the little biddy, staying for a few seconds and then slides off as the biddy moves. Now this looks like serious biddy game time.

Their little bodies are finally tired and the biddies are ready for a nap. Since they do not have a mother hen to get under for protection and warmth, they huddle together in the corner of the box. Their bodies are warm and they like to snuggle together. Mama B keeps a close watch on them when they are tiny. She has a fresh stack of newspapers nearby and changes the newspaper often.

TWO WEEKS OLD

The three little Silkies are about two inches in height and they are little balls of fuzz. They have names: CharCoal is the blue-gray, SnowBall is the white, and ZimBa is the black. They are energetic little biddies and are always jumping on the edge of the cardboard box, trying to escape.

Mama B thinks all of them will grow up to be hens. The lady at Tylertown Farm Supply told her the Silkie biddies were all female and Mama B has no reason to think otherwise. When baby chicks are bought at the store they are sold as straight run, which means that you take what you get. Since the sex of a baby chick is hard to tell until they are much older, a straight run could include both male and female chicks—all male chicks, or all female chicks. SnowBall and CharCoal are about the same size and ZimBa is a little larger. They all appear to be healthy biddies.

They look like they are walking around balancing a cotton ball.

The two Polish biddies have a little puff of white fuzz on top of their head. They look like they are walking around balancing a cotton

ZimBa, SnowBall, and CharCoal strike a pose.

ball. Their bodies are covered with shiny black feathers and they are growing faster than the Silkies since they will be larger when fully grown. One of the Polish biddies is a little larger than the other. Since roosters are larger than hens, this tells Mama B she may have a pair—a rooster and a hen. She will have to be patient and wait awhile to be sure. Since Mama B does not yet know the sex of these biddies, she is going to wait to select names for them.

FOUR WEEKS OLD

The biddies are growing and need more room to run and play. Papa Doc has built a wire chicken coop to replace their cardboard box. The coop is on legs about three feet high. He placed wood dowels on the inside from one side of the coop to the other about eight inches above the floor of the coop. The biddies jump on and off these miniature roost poles and flutter their wings. They are learning to fly by exercising their wings.

Mama B places a pan of sand in the corner of the coop. She watches as the biddies scratch and peck in the sand. They eat some of the grains of sand. The sand collects inside their gizzard where it grinds the food and aids their digestion.

The biddies enjoy lying down on their side in the sand, flapping their wings, and scratching in the dirt, then using their beak to fluff their feathers. This seemingly untidy behavior puts a mixture of dust and sand on their skin and feathers and is called dusting. It is nature's way of preventing mites from getting on chickens.

Since the coop has a wire floor, cleaning up is much easier for Mama B. The mess falls through the wire onto the dirt floor of the chicken house. The grown chickens eat any food that falls through the wire. By now the biddies have learned everything they need to know without the instructions of a mother hen—or even Mama B.

This little Polish biddy is fun to photograph.

SIX WEEKS OLD

The biddies are now too big for the little chicken coop and are ready to roost with the other chickens. Mama B is amazed at how quickly the biddies have grown from the little balls of fuzz she bought at Tylertown Farm Supply only a few weeks before. Mama B got her wish, as it is now apparent that the White Crested Black Polish chickens are indeed a pair, a rooster and a young hen (also known as a pullet). Mama B is going to name them Mr. and Mrs. Whitehead.

A photo of baby Mr. Whitehead

The Silkies—CharCoal, SnowBall, and ZimBa—are very affectionate. They come to Mama B and want to be picked up and cuddled when she is in the chicken yard. She often holds them and talks to them. They respond with their own little chicken talk and coo back to Mama B as if they know what she is saying.

Mama B believes the clerk at Tylertown Farm Supply was correct in telling her that the three chicks are all little hens. Oh, but she is in for a surprise.

Their silky feathers are getting thicker. When they are grown, their feathers will be soft down and feel like hair. The feathers will grow on their legs and feet as well as their body. Mama B believes the clerk at Tylertown Farm Supply was correct in telling her that the three chicks are all little hens. Oh, but she is in for a surprise.

It is early in the morning and Mama B and Papa Doc are having their coffee, sitting in their rocking chairs on the front porch. The birds are singing as the beautiful sunrise stretches and grows, climbing above the treetops on the hillside. Bo is waiting patiently for Mama B to go to the chicken house. Three bluebirds are in the birdbath taking their morning bath. Another is perched on the side, drinking water. A pair of cardinals that were at the feeder eating sunflower seeds have joined the bluebirds at the birdbath. The blue feathers of the bluebirds and the red feathers of the cardinals are brilliant with the bright morning sun shining on them.

The roosters are crowing, one after the other. Mama B recognizes the crow of the Bantams and Mr. Whitehead but hears another crow she cannot recognize. "That rooster has a lot of practicing to do," Mama B tells Papa Doc as she puts on her outside chicken yard shoes and her bonnet. She has to feed the chickens and while she is in the chicken yard, maybe that rooster with the squeaky crow voice will crow again and she can see just who is making such a strange noise.

SnowBall and CharCoal are in the corner of the chicken yard with the other chickens scratching in a pile of pine straw. As Mama B goes in through the chicken yard gate and begins feeding the chickens, she turns toward the roost in the chicken yard and sees ZimBa standing straight and tall on the roost. It is now clear to Mama B that ZimBa is no female. Mama B realizes happily that the Silkie family is made up of one rooster and two pullets. She watches with the love and pride of a true mother as ZimBa holds his neck stretched high in the air attempting to produce his best crow for Mama B. She is pleased with ZimBa even though he still has much work to do on his crow.

ZimBa comes into his own.

The roosters are crowing, one after the other. Mama B recognizes the crow of the Bantams and Mr. Whitehead but hears another crow she cannot recognize. "That rooster has a lot of practicing to do."

This family of biddies has grown up and Mama B finally has her flock of assorted chickens with different personalities. She misses not having the little biddies and unless he wants even more chickens on the farm, next spring Papa Doc had better go to Tylertown Farm Supply by himself and leave Mama B at home. We all know that if Mama B goes, there will always be chickens, chickens, and more chickens on Bluebird Hill.

The Big Fat White Chicken

The Bradford pear tree is covered in white flowers announcing another springtime on Bluebird Hill. Mama B and Papa Doc enjoy their farm as it awakens from winter to a season of new beginnings, a season of baby birds, and of course to Mama B, a season of baby chicks.

Mama B would like to have a few standard-size, plain old chickens to add to her flock of mostly small chickens. She has already surprised Papa Doc with more biddies after promising not to add any more to the flock. But this time, she talked things over with him and he understands her reasons for adding just a few more biddies. The new standard-size chickens would sing louder, crow louder, and the hens would produce larger eggs. They, of course, eat more food than the little Bantams but Mama B would like an assortment of different chickens in her flock. This is a hobby for her. Mama B only uses the eggs her chickens produce and couldn't possibly think of raising the chickens for food.

One stop at Tylertown Farm Supply is all Mama B needs to choose her new biddies. But the decision turns out to be hard to makebecause there are several different breeds and sizes to choose from. The five-day-old biddies are very noisy and busy eating their food of chick

LIVE BABY CHICKS

starter and drinking water. They raise their heads and look at Mama B as she enters the room. Mama B imagines them saying, *Please take me home with you to Bluebird Hill.*

"Let's see," says Mama B, "I want one Giant Black (black), two Barred Plymouth Rocks (black-and-white), one Rhode Island Red (red), and the large white one at the feeder." Five new baby chicks of different colors should be a good assortment for right now, she decides. The nice man in the feed store puts the biddies in the usual biddy box, a small square box with little round holes cut out on the sides for ventilation. Mama B pays her bill and is out of the store and on her way back to the farm in no time at all. The little biddies are noisy and peck the inside of the box as they travel to their new home on Bluebird Hill. As soon as Mama B arrives home, she places the biddies in a large cardboard box with layers of newspaper as their floor. A watering jug and a feeder filled with chick starter complete their nursery. Until they get a little older and the days get a little warmer, they will remain in their box in the barn.

Mama B watches as the biddies finish eating their food. Next they gather in the corner of the box and stand on their tippy-toes to snuggle together for warmth and go to sleep. Mama B covers the box with an old towel and the biddies sleep through the night.

The next morning the newspaper is a big mess. Mama B adds fresh newspaper, food, and fresh clean water. The little ones seem happy. They have immediately scratched their food out of the feeder onto the clean newspaper. But that's all right, Mama B has a big stack of newspaper waiting just for them. They are jumping on top of the water jug and on top of each other. They peck the toes and beak of one another. They are exercising their wings by trying to fly out of the box. They are very active, healthy little biddies.

Even as a young biddie, the white one always ate more and was less active than the others.

TWO WEEKS OLD

The biddies are growing fast and need a larger place. The white biddy, chosen to add the purity of white to the flock, is much larger than the others. Mama B is puzzled by its constant eating and concerned about its rapid growth.

The chicken coop will be the biddies' home for the next few weeks. The coop is a pen completely enclosed with wire. It stands on four legs and has a tin roof. The biddies can see out and today, with the sun shining on one side of the coop, two of the biddies are enjoying the warmth by lying down in the sun with their wings stretched out. Two others are jumping up and down, practicing their flying. All the biddies are very noisy and active except the white one. She is busy eating and drinking.

SIX WEEKS OLD

The biddies are outgrowing the coop. They are beginning to get their permanent feathers and instead of little balls of fuzz, they now look like chickens. It is time for them to take another step and learn how to roost with the other chickens. They have been communicating with the grown-up birds through the wire of the coop and now it's time for a proper meeting. There is much excitement as Mama B opens the door on top of the coop. This is the day they have been waiting for. It is a day of freedom. Mama B can't help but laugh as she watches the biddies jump, one after the other, on top of the coop and fly down to the ground. They jump up into the air just to see how high they can go. It's fun to watch them all having a good time—all but the white chicken. She is busy eating her new food of cracked corn and chicken scratch. Well, perhaps she is happy too.

> This is the day they've been waiting for. It is a day of freedom.

The older chickens stand back and watch. They have never seen anything like this. The biddies that have been living in the coop above their heads are now on the ground with them and they look totally different. *Who are these five lively little things that seem to be taking over their territory?* The older chickens hold their heads high in the air, turning sideways for a closer look. They are probably wondering just how long this visit with the biddies will last or if the newcomers have moved in permanently.

Studying them, Mama B sees that four of the biddies are the size of the full-grown Bantams, but the white chicken—oh, that white chicken—is much larger than the Bantams and is outgrowing all the

Mama B worries endlessly about the white chicken.

other chickens, even the Giant Black who shares her birthday.

As Mama B leaves the chicken yard, she looks back and sees all the chickens eating together. They seem to be adapting well and getting along just fine. Sometimes when new chickens are mixed for the first time they peck and chase each other. New chickens are not always welcome in an established chicken house flock.

It is getting dark and Mama B makes a final trip out to the chicken house to see if the new residents of the chicken house have found the roost. She is a little concerned because they did not have a mother hen to teach them about the roost. Yes, she sees that those smart little chickens are on the roost. And guess who is on the highest roost pole in the chicken house? Yes, the white chicken has made her way up and found herself the perfect spot for the night. She has chosen the roosting spot right in the middle of the Bantams. The other four biddies are on the end of the roost snuggled close together.

FIVE MONTHS OLD

The roosters begin crowing before daylight. Mama B and Papa Doc are used to the pre-dawn serenades and awaken on their own shortly

Daybreak on Bluebird Hill

after first light. Mama B is in the kitchen making a pot of coffee. She is anxious to get the coffee brewed so that she can take her cup and sit on the porch to watch the birds, and listen to the roosters crow. The glow of the sun rising in the east over the tips of the pine trees is a show in itself. The sounds of nature that surround her make getting up early in the morning on Bluebird Hill well worth the effort.

While sipping her coffee, Mama B watches the crows squabbling as they fly from limb to limb in a nearby pecan tree. They are probably fussing over an old pecan.

The cardinals are the first birds to come to the feeder early in the morning. The male cardinal is red with a black patch at the base of his red bill. The female is light brown with some red on her wings and tail. With the sun shining on their feathers, the birds appear even brighter.

Suddenly Mama B's attention turns to the chickens. There is a loud commotion in the chicken yard and it sounds as if a chicken is in trouble. Mama B puts her coffee cup down and is in the chicken yard in a flash. She sees a Bantam rooster, with white feathers in his mouth, chasing the white chicken. The white chicken is so fat she can hardly run or fly to get away from him. By the time Mama B gets inside the chicken yard, however, the Bantam rooster has for some reason given up his attack on the white chicken and has picked a fight with Mr. Speckle, a pretty black-and-white rooster twice his size.

Rooster fights are relatively tame, especially since Mama B has trimmed the roosters' spurs to keep them from hurting each other. She uses a broom to break up the fight, and puts the roosters in separate chicken yards to cool off for a while. In spite of the occasional misbehavior, roosters are important to the flock for many reasons—

not the least of which is that they are the chickens' ala
When a rooster sees a hawk fly overhead, he looks up to
makes an unusual sound telling all the chickens there is
all stop what they are doing and stand very still. Wh
starts moving again, he is signaling all-clear and it's back to bus
as usual.

An important part of life in the chicken house is the production of farm-fresh eggs from the hens. It is, of course, a huge deal when a hen lays an egg in the nest in the chicken house. The celebration involves all the residents and it's noisy and joyful. The five new pul-

A mismatched rooster fight

lets—soon to be hens—are not sure what the party is all about. They stretch their heads high as they witness the reveling, but they do not make a sound. It will not be long before the Rhode Island Red, Barred Plymouth Rocks, and Black Giant hens reach maturity and begin laying eggs. They will be cackling over their own big brown eggs. The white chicken, of course, will be producing white eggs.

It is late in the afternoon and roost time again. But this time, the white chicken cannot get on the roost. She is so heavy that when she jumps on the chicken walk, she falls off. She tries to fly to a lower pole and cannot even fly that high. She cannot get off the ground. When she tries, flop, she goes right down onto the chicken house floor. Dust and straw fly everywhere in a big puff, then settle back on the ground. Eventually she stops trying to get onto the roost. She knows Mama B will come out to pick her up. Mama B has rescued her before and she will do it again. On this night Mama B puts her on the roost with her four close chicken

> It is, of course, a huge deal when a hen lays an egg in the nest in the chicken house. The celebration involves all the residents and it's noisy and joyful.

friends. But just as Mama B is walking out of the chicken house, she hears a loud noise and turns just in time to see the big fat white chicken lose her balance and fall to the ground once again. One more time Mama B picks the big fat white chicken up and puts her back on the roost. She holds her steady for a minute to be sure she will stay put for the night. Mama B walks quickly out of the chicken house hoping for the best.

Chickens prefer the safety of the highest roost pole.

SIX MONTHS OLD

It is a hot day in August and the big fat white chicken is still eating constantly. But on this particular hot day she is having trouble breathing. She is sitting on the ground with her wings spread out and her mouth open, trying to breathe. She is in trouble. She cannot run fast enough to get away from the other chickens that chase her. Few feathers remain on her rump as the other chickens have plucked them.

When a chicken is hurt or sick, other chickens will continue to peck or hurt the weakened one—possibly in an effort to put the creature out of its misery. Mama B has a suspicion about the big fat white chicken and after some research and a phone call, it is confirmed. That pretty little white biddy was bred to become a big fat white chicken—fat, succulent, and yes, might as well tell it like it is—delicious. But Mama B cannot think about cooking the big fat white chicken even if it does fulfill what she was bred to do. Mama B doesn't care what she was bred to do, that big fat white chicken is Mama B's beloved pet.

Living on a farm, however, does force you to be a realist and Mama B knows that if she doesn't do something, that poor chicken will die a terrible death right in the chicken yard. After much soul searching, she decides to ask several of her farm neighbors if they would like to have a good fat chicken. But to her surprise, farmer after farmer say the same thing: "Thank you just the same, Mama B, but we don't use fresh chickens anymore since we can buy them cheap at the grocery store and ready to cook."

What is Mama B going to do? The big fat white chicken has broken two roost poles in the chicken house trying to fly up on the roost. Mama B told Papa Doc to replace the poles with sturdier poles that will hold an eight-pound chicken. Whatever will become of the big fat white chicken? Mama B worries day and night. She will not give up but will try, one more time, to find someone who will take the big fat white chicken.

At last Mama B does find someone. The Heberts are very happy to have a fresh fat chicken. Miss Sue enjoys cooking, and gumbo— chicken gumbo— is one of her favorite things to cook.

Before Miss Sue comes to get the big fat white chicken, Mama B feeds her one last time with freshly shelled cracked corn and water. Miss Sue arrives with a box with clean newspaper in the bottom. Mama B sprinkles a little chicken scratch and cracked corn on the newspaper, and the big fat white chicken is gone.

The next day Miss Sue calls Mama B to thank her for her gift of the big fat white chicken. "Yes, my love," Miss Sue tells her, "that big fat white chicken was a big chicken. She dressed over seven pounds." This means the big fat white chicken weighed eight pounds or more fully feathered.

Mama B is sad because she enjoyed watching the big fat white chicken through her life span. But she finds comfort in knowing that the white biddy turned into a big fat white chicken just as she was bred to do. Of course, Mama B had helped a lot by feeding her so much.

Now when Mama B hears a commotion in the chicken house she thinks of her favorite white biddy who needed her help. She will remember that she must always question the breed of a white chicken. Next time she will ask for a White Leghorn, a small hardy chicken that produces eggs prolifically.

Suddenly, a loud cackle from the chicken house notifies Mama B that the other four hens are laying big brown eggs. They are doing what they were bred to do—lay eggs.

The big fat white chicken

MAMA B'S CHICKEN GUMBO

Mama B does not cook her chickens. When she wants to make chicken gumbo, she buys a chicken at the grocery store, dressed and ready for the pot. And then she follows this recipe (ingredients listed to the right and directions on page 60).

INGREDIENT LIST
FOR MAMA B'S CHICKEN GUMBO

1 WHOLE CHICKEN CUT INTO PIECES
(OR 4 QUARTERS)

3 CHICKEN BOUILLON CUBES

1 TEASPOON BLACK PEPPER

1 CUP CHOPPED CELERY

1 CUP CHOPPED GREEN BELL PEPPER

1 CUP CHOPPED ONION

1 CUP SLICED OKRA

½ CUP VEGETABLE OIL

½ CUP ALL-PURPOSE FLOUR

1 TABLESPOON DRY PARSLEY FLAKES

1 TABLESPOON TONY CHACHERE'S
CREOLE SEASONING MIX

1 TEASPOON CAVENDER'S GREEK SEASONING

DASH OF THYME

2 CLOVES GARLIC, CHOPPED
(OR 1 TEASPOON GARLIC POWDER)

8 INCHES SMOKED SAUSAGE, SLICED THIN

2 FOURTEEN-OUNCE CANS DICED TOMATOES

WHITE RICE

MAMA B'S CHICKEN GUMBO

Ingredient list on previous page

Wash chicken in cool water and boil in a covered pot with enough water to cover meat. Add bouillon cubes and pepper. Boil until meat is fork tender, about 40 minutes. Reserve broth.

While the chicken is cooking, make a roux. Yes, you can do it!

Roux

Pour oil in a large heavy skillet. When the oil is hot, add flour, stirring constantly on medium heat. Do not burn, adjusting heat accordingly. Cook and stir until the color of peanut butter. Add bell pepper, celery, onion, and okra to roux mixture. Cook on medium heat, stirring and turning to keep from sticking. This will take about 20 minutes. Vegetables will be tender and mixture will be medium brown in color when finished.

When the chicken in the pot is tender (easily pierced with a fork), remove chicken from the broth and let cool. When cool enough to handle, discard skin and remove chicken from bones. Discard bones. Cut chicken into bite-size pieces.

If you cook the chicken the day before and the broth has been in the refrigerator, the fat will come to the top and you can skim it off and discard. (Usually I am not this far ahead, so I am trying to get the fat off while the broth is hot and this is what I figured out and it works for me.)

Take a quart jar and carefully ladle the hot broth into the jar (don't burn yourself). The fat will come to the top (mouth) of the jar. Scoop it out with a spoon and put it in a cup lined with a paper towel. When finished, discard paper towel that has absorbed the fat.

Put the chicken broth (1 quart – add a little water if needed) and the pieces of chicken back in the pot. If the roux mixture has finished cooking, add it now. Add parsley, Tony's, Cavender's, garlic, thyme, sausage and tomatoes. Simmer on low 30 minutes, stirring occasionally. If too thick, add a little water.

Taste to check flavor—your decision: if you want it hotter to taste, add a little red pepper or Louisiana Hot Sauce. Add salt and black pepper if desired. Simmer another 10 minutes.

Serve over a bed of white rice cooked as package directs.

Enjoy!

From the kitchen of Mama B.

The little red rooster

The Love of a Mother Hen

Evening is falling and it's roost time for the older chickens on Bluebird Hill. They seem to love the cozy chicken house that Papa Doc built for them. He put in good, strong poles for roosting, which, in the world of fowl, is their way of sleeping. And he even designed a clever chicken walk so that the smallest biddies can get up to the first roost pole with a short flight or jump from board to board.

The little Bantam mother welcomes her biddies to the roost.

These biddies are four weeks old and so far they have been sleeping on the ground beneath their mother, a little Bantam hen. But now the mother hen is getting restless as she sees the other grown-up chickens go to roost. Her chicken instinct tells her it is time for her and her biddies to leave their little nursery and roost on the roost poles with the older chickens.

Mama B is peeking through the fence on this particular evening, watching and listening as, one by one, the older chickens fly to the highest roost pole in the chicken house. The little mother hen is clucking fast and loud as she approaches the chicken walk with her biddies following close behind her. The little hen stands near the chicken walk and looks up to the first roost pole. She squats flat on the ground, spreads her wings out, and flies up to the first roost pole.

Sitting on the roost pole and looking down, the mother hen clucks even louder and faster to her biddies on the ground. She nods her head up and down while clucking as she moves around on the pole. She clucks in varying tones, clearly urging her biddies to come up to the roost. On the ground, the little biddies are chirping pitifully to their mother hen, most likely saying, But Mama, we can't fly that high. Our tiny wings won't let us. Please come back down and let us sleep cozy under your warm feathers.

But the wise mother hen knows that, difficult as it may be, she has to stand firm up on the roost to teach her biddies how to be proper chickens that sleep on a roost. After a good deal of fussing, the little biddies finally try to do as their mother showed them. They squat on the ground, flap their wings, and up they go in the air toward the first roost pole where their mother is anxiously prancing back and forth. But each time they try, they miss. Up they go, again and again, one or two at a time, each one missing the pole by a few inches and falling back to the ground. It's hard to tell who's becoming more anxious—the little mother hen or Mama B.

Mama B breathes a sigh of relief when finally one smart little biddy discovers Papa Doc's chicken walk.

But the biddies keep trying, the mother hen keeps urging, and Mama B breathes a sigh of relief when finally one smart little biddy discovers Papa Doc's chicken walk. Now they will all realize this is the easy way to reach their mother hen without a long-distance flight.

With little effort the biddies fly or jump to the first board of the chicken walk. The mother hen is calmly watching each biddy's success.

Now her clucks have changed from anxious and insistent to a softer tone. She seems to be saying, yes, yes, yes, as each of her biddies come closer to her warm, feathered body. Mama B is thrilled to see that once they are all together the little ones celebrate in happy, chirping chatter, while the mother hen is calmly praising and encouraging them with soft clucks.

The happy chicken family continues its little chat with soft chirps as the tiny biddies settle for the night, under the comfort of the mother hen's warm wings. Now the chicken chatter grows softer and softer as the drowsy biddies nod off one by one, and the mother hen, pleased by the accomplishments of her brood, joins them in sleep.

Mama B walks away quietly, savoring the experience and privilege of once again seeing the love of a mother hen on Bluebird Hill. She knows that few people have the opportunity to witness such tenderness in the animal world.

A Surprise in the Chicken House

It is a cool spring morning on Bluebird Hill, and the fruit trees are beginning to bud. That means it is time for Papa Doc to spray the orchard in hopes of good fresh fruit to eat this summer. Without spraying, the worms will eat more fruit than Mama B and Papa Doc. The Bluebird Hill orchard boasts apple, pear, plum, apricot, blueberry, quince, persimmon, and crab apple trees.

Bo is in the orchard with Papa Doc when he comes upon a mouse in the grass. He jumps up and down trying to get his paws on the mouse. Mama B, who is on her way to the chicken house, chuckles when she sees his white-tipped tail bobbing up and down. The mouse scurries into a hole and Bo scratches at the hole but quickly gives up, graciously handing the mouse a nice victory.

When Mama B turns her attention to her chickens in the chicken yard, she sees Rufus, her colorful Bantam rooster, dancing around a yellow-speckled Bantam hen. Rufus is trying to get the little hen's attention away from a rival rooster. He moves around her in circles, dropping his wing, until the tip touches the ground. Rufus's mating dance succeeds in capturing the little hen's attention as she comes close and turns her head to get a better look at her suitor.

Bradford pear tree

Mama B notices that CharCoal, her favorite little hen, is not out in the chicken yard. CharCoal is a beautiful old Silkie Bantam hen. She is blue-gray in color and so tame and friendly that she likes to be picked up and loved. Her cuddly feathers feel like soft fluffy hair. Mama B enjoys holding CharCoal close as they carry on a conversation. Mama B often tells CharCoal what a wonderful little friend she is and CharCoal talks back with her cooing chicken sounds.

Mama B opens the gate and goes into the chicken yard, hoping to find CharCoal. While she is feeding the chickens, she notices CharCoal

Romance in the chicken yard.

CharCoal is an independent little hen—a true modern woman.

inside the chicken house sitting on a nest. Since CharCoal was on that same nest the day before, it looks as if the little hen is getting the motherly instinct and is setting.

Mama B lifts CharCoal off the nest just long enough to see five tiny Bantam eggs. The eggs were laid by other Bantam hens not interested in setting at the time. This is not at all unusual, as a chicken will set on eggs that are not her own if she desires to become a mother. CharCoal has taken advantage of an opportunity to make a dream come true, in spite of her advanced age and the fact that she has not laid an egg in two years. Mama B knows of CharCoal's desire because her little hen has been showing signs of wanting to set by getting on and off the nest. That is not to say that she has been clucking and preparing herself as hens usually do before nesting. But CharCoal is different from the other chickens. She does not socialize or eat with the other chickens. When Rufus, the Bantam rooster clucks his calling, first low and then louder, to invite his lady friends to share a treat or to dine on a cricket or a bug, all the girls come running except CharCoal. She continues scratching in the corner of the chicken yard all by herself, looking for her own cricket. She is an independent little hen—a true modern woman.

Mama B rubs CharCoal's tiny head and whispers to her, "If you really want to set on the eggs and raise some biddies, I will help you do just that. But, CharCoal, you need to be sure this is really what you want to do. It is a big step for a little old Silkie hen to have the responsibility of biddies."

CharCoal shifts around in the nest and settles back down on the warm eggs. She seems to be very certain about wanting to become a mother. "Okay, little mother," says Mama B, "let's do it!"

Mama B keeps a close watch on CharCoal most of the day to see if she is still on the nest in the afternoon. As the sun begins to lower in the western sky and Mama B sees that CharCoal has not moved from the nest, she decides to add a few more Bantam eggs. This will give CharCoal a good setting of eggs.

Just before dark, Mama B goes in the farmhouse and marks six Bantam eggs with a marker. She places the marked eggs and the marker in her egg basket and carries them to the chicken house. When she gets to the chicken house she will also mark the eggs that are under CharCoal before adding the six eggs she marked earlier.

Mama B is off to the chicken house.

With the eggs marked, she will be able to identify a new egg laid in the nest and remove it. This is a necessary step because all the eggs need to be set on for the same length of time so they will hatch close to the same time. That will free the mother hen from having to set on the nest and she can then devote her attention to caring for her biddies.

The eggs with biddies in them will hatch in twenty-one days and Mama B will throw away the eggs that do not hatch.

With the basket of eggs in hand and Bo following close behind, Mama B stops on the porch to put on her bonnet and chicken yard shoes that she left on the porch earlier. Off they go, walking side by side to the chicken house.

When they get to the chicken yard, Mama B opens the gate and Bo stands back. He knows that he is not allowed in the chicken yard or the chicken house. Mama B can see CharCoal from the gate and she is not setting on the nest. She is on the bottom roost pole looking down into the nest. All the other chickens are on the top roost poles in the chicken house, and they all have their eyes on CharCoal.

"Well," Mama B whispers to herself, "perhaps she is just not really ready to be the mother of biddies. It's disappointing but looks like she has gone to roost with the other chickens for the night."

When Mama B gets in the chicken house she stoops to get under the first roost pole where CharCoal is perched with her wings spread out from her body for balance. CharCoal is clucking loudly and seems upset. Mama B stands between CharCoal and the nest, close enough to the nest so that she can touch the eggs and see if they are warm.

Charcoal is off the nest and her companions seem concerned.

If the eggs are still warm, it may simply mean that CharCoal took a brief break and would be returning shortly.

Just as Mama B looks over in the nest, and is ready to put her hand on the eggs, she sees that instead of the tiny eggs, there is a chicken snake in the nest. Mama B gasps and jumps back quickly.

She knows that a chicken snake will not bother her, but she does not like snakes of any kind. A chicken snake will get in a chicken house and swallow the eggs whole. And though they cannot eat a whole grown chicken, they can eat a baby chick.

Mama B runs back to the farmhouse still clutching the basket of eggs tightly, with Bo running ahead of her. Since Bo didn't see the snake, he doesn't know exactly what is going on but he senses that Mama B is upset.

"Put your book down, Papa Doc, and come to the chicken house with me," Mama B yells. "There is a chicken snake in CharCoal's nest!" Mama B carefully places her basket of eggs on the kitchen table and hurries out the door after Papa Doc who is already rushing to the barn to get a hoe. Mama B and Bo wait just outside the chicken yard. In no time, Papa Doc returns with the hoe and that sets Bo off. He jumps up and down, barking and trying his best to get away from

> "Put your book down, Papa Doc, and come to the chicken house with me," Mama B yells. "There is a chicken snake in CharCoal's nest!"

Mama B, who is holding his collar with both hands as Papa Doc hurries into the chicken house.

Now, the chicken house is Mama B's territory and the chickens know it. So when the chickens see Papa Doc enter the chicken house with the hoe, they fly off the roost, heading in all directions in a squawking, clucking, dusty, screeching panic. Strangely, the chickens are not afraid of the snake, they are afraid of Papa Doc. Papa Doc knows that if he just holds still a bit, the commotion will end. When it does, the flock re-groups in the far corner of the chicken yard as Papa Doc raises his hoe and walks slowly over to the nest. Just before he gets close enough to strike at the snake, it slithers out of the nest and falls onto the dirt floor of the chicken house. It starts toward Papa Doc, then changes direction and slithers under the back wall of the chicken house to the outside. Mama B, Bo, and all the chickens watch as Papa Doc comes running out of the chicken house holding the hoe up in the air. He is afraid of the snake and the snake is afraid of Papa Doc.

Papa Doc gives chase but the snake is too fast for him.

Papa Doc runs through the chicken yard, out the gate, and around to the back of the chicken house. But by the time he gets there, the snake has disappeared into the briar patch behind the chicken house. Mama B knows that the cowardly snake will probably never return to the chicken house. But she also knows the snake did not leave hungry because it ate all of the little eggs that were under CharCoal.

With the snake out of the chicken house, the chickens can now have a quiet night's sleep on the roost. Papa Doc, Mama B, and Bo go back to the farmhouse. Mama B thinks about CharCoal, wondering if she will get back on the nest.

The following morning Mama B is anxious to get to the chicken house to see about CharCoal. Yes, CharCoal is on the nest, which doesn't have a single egg in it. What a determined little hen. Well, Mama B knows a thing or two about determination and off she goes back to the farmhouse to get the basket of eggs she was going to put under CharCoal the night before. When she places them gently under the little hen, CharCoal moves her body around in the nest and settles down on the six tiny eggs. She is ready to start over and commit to the twenty-one-day countdown. Mama B is excited for CharCoal and happy to help her make her dream come true.

nineteen days

CharCoal is off the nest when Mama B gets to the chicken house to feed the chickens. The eggs are a little cool and Mama B is concerned. CharCoal has almost reached her goal—why would she get off now? But in a few minutes CharCoal goes back on the nest. "CharCoal," Mama B chides, "with this going on, we may not have any biddies." CharCoal settles herself on the nest and makes no response.

twenty-one days

Mama B's chicken yard shoes

This is the day on which CharCoal's biddies should be hatching. Mama B puts on her chicken yard shoes and heads for the chicken house thinking about the many trips she has made to see about her favorite little feathered friend. It has been a hard time for CharCoal, but she has handled it well. Mama B occasionally saw her off the nest just long enough to eat and drink. But after a short break the little hen always went back to her eggs.

It is a gloomy day with light rain falling and Mama B is a little later than usual going to the chicken house. As she nears the chicken house she believes she hears the sound of a biddy. Its tiny voice sounds frightened. Mama B sees the fuzzy little yellow creature in the nest alone, with three unhatched eggs. CharCoal is on the floor of the chicken house with two other biddies. She has made a nest with pine straw on the dirt floor. The biddies are under her wings with their heads sticking out to see what is going on. They get their first look at Mama B and

Mama B gets her first look at them. This is an exciting day for all.

The safety of her biddies is CharCoal's main concern. When the two biddies jumped out of the nest, CharCoal jumped after them. She was afraid the other chickens would harm them. She knew the little biddy in the nest with the eggs would be safe until Mama B got to the chicken house.

Mama B puts CharCoal and the biddies back in the nest with the other little biddy. She goes to the barn, gets the chicken coop, and sets it up in the chicken house. She fills the water jar with fresh water and fills the feeder with chick starter food. She places the water jar in the corner of the coop. Next she puts newspaper on the wire floor of the coop and places the feeder on the newspaper. The newspaper keeps most of the food from falling through the wire onto the dirt floor.

She puts CharCoal and her three biddies in the coop and smiles as CharCoal immediately begins teaching her little biddies to eat the chick starter by putting some in her mouth and dropping it onto the newspaper. She pecks the food on the newspaper and the tiny biddies imitate her. This is their first of many lessons.

CharCoal has her three fluffy biddies to raise and she seems to be happy with her new family. They are tiny little balls of fuzz, about one inch high. They burrow under CharCoal's wings and stick their heads out from beneath her feathers. One is yellow, one is blue-gray, and the other is speckled with different colors.

CharCoal is clucking and the biddies are talking back to her in their baby chick talk. Mama B stands close by, wondering just what they are saying to each other. She thinks that perhaps CharCoal is telling them that not even a snake could keep her from being a mom.

Rufus the rooster and all the chickens are looking around with great curiosity. They are holding their heads up high and turning their necks sideways, trying to see what is going on in the chicken coop above their heads and why CharCoal is getting so much special attention.

The next morning the biddies seem to have grown overnight. The yellow biddie is standing in the water and drinking. The blue-gray and speckled ones are pecking food in keeping with CharCoal's instructions. CharCoal is giving them first-hand advice with her clucking on just what to do and what not to do. Mama B realizes that triplets were

Mama B thinks that perhaps CharCoal is telling them that not even a snake could keep her from being a mom.

just right for CharCoal. Sextuplets would have been far too many biddies for the little old Silkie hen to handle.

four weeks later

This day is going to be a growing-up day for CharCoal's biddies. They are going to find out what it is like living with the other chickens. It's roost time and Mama B takes CharCoal out of the coop and places her on the dirt floor of the chicken house.

Since they are old enough to roost, the biddies are old enough to be named. Mama B likes to call all her chickens by name and talk to them. The blue-gray will be Silver Chic; the yellow is named Daf-O-Dil; and the multicolored, Spec. CharCoal has one little pullet that will grow up to be a hen, and two little roosters. Spec and Silver Chic are the roosters. They are a little larger than the pullet. Their red combs have started growing on top of their head. Spec's feathers of many colors resemble those of Rufus, his daddy.

Before Mama B can stand up straight after putting CharCoal on the floor of the chicken house, Silver Chic and Daf-O-Dil see the opening above their heads. They are anxious to get out of the coop, and with a few flutters of their wings they fly up and land on top of the coop. A few seconds later Spec is right by their sides. From the edge of the coop they peer down at CharCoal with the look of *what next?*

Mama B stands back to watch. All three fly off the coop and land near CharCoal. It is about a three-foot flight from the top of the coop to the chicken house dirt floor. Their little wings are strong enough to give them a soft dusty landing. They continue to jump up in the air and fly a short distance, enjoying their freedom.

CharCoal has a busy day teaching her biddies about the chicken yard, the chicken house, and living with other chickens. She scratches in the dirt for bugs or seeds and notifies her biddies by clucking when she finds one. She first clucks soft and slow, then fast and louder, as she moves her head up and down, pecking where she has found something to eat. The little biddies have learned well and come running when she clucks. They also have learned that the first one to arrive gets the goodie.

CharCoal scratches a round hole in the dirt of the chicken yard about the size of her body to make a bed of dust. She gets in the dusty hole and flaps her wings as she moves her body. Her feathers fluff out as she scratches dust all over her body. She turns one way and then the other as she continues to scratch and flap her wings. She uses her beak to move her feathers around so that dust can get on her skin. Dust-

CharCoal is a good little mother who enjoys introducing her biddies to the world.

ing is nature's way to keep chickens free of mites. This is her biddies' first show-and-tell for the process of dusting. Silver Chic, Daf-O-Dil, and Spec—the triplet biddies—watch closely. CharCoal stands up, shakes off the dust, and fluffs her feathers. The three biddies get in the dust and try to follow the directions CharCoal has given. The biddies find that it is indeed a lot of fun.

CharCoal's personality has changed since she became a mom to the little biddies. She is no longer alone. She has a family. The other chickens are curious about the little biddies and about CharCoal. They come close to investigate, but CharCoal chases them away. The little mother hen sits down on the ground to rest and cuddles her biddies under her body. The two little heads of Silver Chic and Daf-O-Dil are sticking out from under her wings. The third little biddy, Spec, comes out from under the back of CharCoal and jumps on her back. He stands there and looks around. CharCoal stands up and little Spec slides off her back. No rest for CharCoal.

It's almost dark and time for the chickens to go to roost. Did they remember their lessons today about the chicken walk? Mama B is near the chicken house watching to see if the biddies remember. The coop has been removed from the chicken house and stored in the barn. It is the first roost time for Silver Chic, Daf-O-Dil, and Spec.

CharCoal flies up and lands on the roost pole closest to the ground. She jumps up to another pole and then another. She is now on the highest pole with the other chickens. The higher the chickens are on the roost the safer they feel.

CharCoal clucks, and the biddies look up at her as if trying to remember how to get up on the roost. Daf-O-Dil tries to fly to the first pole and misses it by about three inches. Silver Chic tries and lands on the pole but quickly loses his balance and falls off, down to the chicken house floor. Flying lessons have paid off because he at least had a soft landing. Next Spec goes over to the chicken walk. He jumps on the chicken walk and is on the first roost pole in no time at all, flying from one pole to the other. He is showing his little pullet sister and his rooster brother just how it is done. Silver Chic and Daf-O-Dil watch and follow his directions without any problems. In no time, they are all up on the roost with CharCoal.

Their next challenge is trying to figure out how to fit under Char-Coal on the roost and still remain balanced on the pole. They have not had lessons in balancing on the roost and are about to discover that it is not an easy thing to do. But after falling to the chicken house floor several times and jumping on the chicken walk to get back up, they begin to catch on to the art of balancing. The triplets have learned the lesson of roosting. The soft chirping between the mother hen and her biddies subsides. The biddies settle down under the warm wings of their little mother hen for the night and soon all are asleep.

CharCoal has proven herself a good mother to Silver Chic, Daf-O-Dil, and Spec. She did not let the snake or any other problems interfere with her plans. She set her little chicken mind to it and fulfilled her wishes with determination and success.

The Chickens Escape

It is a hot July afternoon on Bluebird Hill. Mama B hears the roar of thunder and the wind is starting to pick up. There is a thunderstorm brewing in the southwest.

Suddenly Mama B remembers she has not fed the chickens today. She puts on her old chicken yard shoes and off she goes, with Bo tagging along behind her, the short distance to the barn. She fills her bucket with chicken scratch and laying mash and hurries to the chicken yard, determined to get the chickens fed before the storm arrives. Bo takes off running around the outside of the chicken yard, barking at the chickens. As long as he is *outside* the chicken yard, the chickens are not afraid of Bo and totally ignore him. Perhaps he is talking to them in a friendly conversation of animal talk that Mama B does not understand.

Mama B fills the feeders with the chicken feed and gathers the eggs. She places the eggs gently in her empty feed bucket. Then she notices that the chickens' water supply is getting low. She puts the bucket of eggs down on the ground and picks up the water can. She opens the gate and walks through just as a gust of wind hits the gate hard enough for her to think the gate is closed. But she didn't really hear it close or look back to make sure it was closed so she would have no way of knowing that the gate did not close completely. Others in the chicken yard, however, are all too aware that the gate is partially open.

Mama B fills the water can at the faucet near the barn and walks back toward the chicken yard. Suddenly she sees Rufus the Bantam rooster, CharCoal the old Silkie hen, and CharCoal's little grown biddy, the Silver Chic, who is now a young rooster, making a daring escape through the gate into the green grass of the outside yard.

Mama B puts the water can down in the grass near the gate about the same time Bo sees the chickens. Mama B is in a little tizzy and isn't thinking clearly when she makes her *shhhhhhhhh* sound to the chickens. In Mama B's chicken language this means *move on, chickens.* And they usually do. The problem is that this is also the signal she gives Bo when she wants him to chase the chickens out of the flower garden.

When Bo hears *shhhhhhhh,* he thinks Mama B wants him to chase the chickens and off he runs full blast with Mama B trying to stop him. But it is too late. Bo's aggressive approach and loud bark has the chickens on the run.

In Mama B's chicken language, *shhhhh* means *move on, chickens.* And they usually do. The problem is that this is also the signal she gives Bo when she wants him to chase the chickens out of the flower garden.

Mama B knows it was her *shhhhh* that caused the whole problem and not Bo. She can't blame him; he is only doing what he was taught to do. Rufus runs as fast as he can back through the gate and into the chicken yard for protection from Bo. CharCoal runs toward the barn as fast as she can move her tiny body. The Silver Chic flies straight up and lands on the wire roof of the chicken yard eight feet up.

With the Silver Chic on the roof, Mama B escorts Bo back to the farmhouse where Papa Doc can supervise him. Now she can focus on her chicken problem and the impending storm without Bo under her feet. One chicken is still running around on the outside of the chicken yard fence, and the other is on the wire rooftop of the chicken yard. The wind is picking up now and Mama B has no time to lose. First, she gets a handful of chicken feed from the feeder and sprinkles it just inside the gate of the chicken yard. Then she props the gate wide open with a piece of wood. The chickens inside the chicken yard are busy scratching, clucking, and eating the food on the ground so they are too busy to notice that the gate is open. Mama B's plan is to keep them busy while she concentrates on getting CharCoal and the Silver Chic inside before the storm rolls in.

Now Mama B takes off after CharCoal out in the yard, trying to shoo her through the gate. But the little Silkie is apparently having too much fun outside. So 'round and 'round the chicken yard go Mama B and CharCoal as they both get a little much-needed exercise. Meanwhile the Silver Chic watches with great interest from his perch on the wire roof. First one way and then the other—here comes CharCoal, there goes Mama B. Time and again CharCoal passes right by the wide-open gate as if she does not see it, with Mama B, of course, hot on her trail.

Mama B is convinced CharCoal is enjoying prancing around the yard and has no concerns about the approaching thunderstorm or her young Silver Chic on the roof. As always, Mama B is doing enough worrying for both of them.

At last, after about six times around the chicken yard, CharCoal finally goes through the gate to eat with the other chickens. She has

The Silver Chic peers longingly through the wire.

forgotten about the Silver Chic, who is pacing back and forth on the wire roof just over her head.

"One down and one to go," Mama B whispers softly. Thank heavens, because Mama B is tired. She has used all her energy chasing CharCoal, trying to beat a fast-approaching thunderstorm. With this on her mind, Mama B is concerned about the Silver Chic. He is special to Mama B because he is CharCoal's little rooster.

Mama B goes to one side of the chicken yard and looks up at the Silver Chic just as a loud boom of thunder sends the little rooster scurrying to the other side. The Silver Chic is frightened to be alone up there in the wind and darkening sky, without the comfort of CharCoal, Daf-O-Dil, and Spec. Mama B is certain that the daring escape and fun adventure outside the gate must now seem like a terrible mistake to the Silver Chic, who is looking forlornly through the wire to the ground below, where all the chickens are busy eating. CharCoal is over to the side of the flock, pecking away with Daf-O-Dil and Spec. The Silver Chic's little rooster brain must be wondering why a jump down through the wire is so impossible.

Mama B moves closer to the Silver Chic and, looking up at him, makes her *shhhhh* sound and gestures with her hands to get the

> The Silver Chic's little rooster brain must be wondering why a jump down through the wire is so impossible.

youngster to fly down. But when the Silver Chic sees Mama B, he bounces across the wire roof farther to the other side. But now when the Silver Chic looks down, he sees his mother hen, CharCoal, on the ground just below and this really upsets him. He paces back and forth, looking down at CharCoal in a most pitiful way. It is obvious that he is trying to find a way back down to the safety of the chicken yard. That escape out the door was definitely not a good idea even if it was with Rufus and his very own mother hen. CharCoal has stopped eating, perhaps because she is too worried about her youngster to eat. She is also tired from running around the chicken yard with Mama B.

Mama B thinks of one more thing to try to get the Silver Chic down off the roof. The wind is blowing hard enough to send leaves and twigs sailing across the yard as Mama B runs to the barn, gets a broom, and hurries back to the chicken yard. From inside the chicken yard Mama B holds the broom up and pushes the wire up and down

Mama B and her broom seem to be confusing the Silver Chic.

with the broom, trying to get the Silver Chic to fly off the roof just as he flew up. But the young rooster does not understand. Up in the air goes the Silver Chic and back down he lands, on the wire roof. The Silver Chic is very frightened and Mama B is making it worse.

At last Mama B realizes that it's the Silver Chic's mother, Char-Coal, who holds the answer. The Silver Chic has to see CharCoal in the grass outside the chicken yard before a flight down to the ground is possible. This has to be the solution Mama B has been seeking.

At last the Silver Chic spots his mother on the grass.

Back into the chicken yard Mama B goes—she must catch CharCoal once again. The catch this time is easy because CharCoal is still tired from her recent runs around the chicken yard. Mama B just reaches down and picks up her cuddly little hen. She places her back out in the green grass of the yard about twenty feet from the gate. The Silver Chic can see CharCoal and CharCoal can see him. That is all it takes— one loud cluck from CharCoal and the Silver Chic flies off the chicken yard roof to be with his mother. Mama B walks quietly over to them and with a low *shhhhhhh, shhhhhh,* she follows both through the gate and into the chicken yard.

The first heavy splatters of rain fall on Mama B as she closes the gate and walks quickly back to the water can she left in the grass near the gate. She places the water can in the chicken yard and picks up the feed bucket containing her eggs, just in time for the afternoon thunderstorm.

Silver Chic, CharCoal, and Rufus appear to be busy telling the other chickens about their great escape, most likely advising them never to try such a thing, especially during an approaching thunderstorm. A loud boom of thunder sends all the chickens running into the chicken house. As the storm grows in intensity, the chickens are all safe inside and Mama B is relieved.

Mama B, Papa Doc, and Bo sit on the porch and listen to the rain pounding on the tin roof of the little farmhouse on Bluebird Hill.

Miss Katie and the Wooden Egg

Miss Katie, a tiny Japanese Bantam hen, is as white as snow except for her tail feathers. The tips look like they have been dipped in black paint. The feathers on her tail fold together and stand up in the back. This petite little hen struts around the chicken yard as if she does not want to get one speck of dirt on her pretty white feathers. She knows she is a cutie and she is a determined little setter, as are most Bantam hens.

Miss Katie is both beautiful and fastidious.

Miss Katie, so named by Mama B for her dear mother who is now in Heaven, has been clucking and sitting on the same nest for a few days. Mama B has decided to quit taking the eggs from under Miss Katie every day and allow her to set, which means keeping the little eggs warm so that they can hatch into

It's important to understand that the eggs Miss Katie has been setting on are eggs from other hens since a setting hen stops laying eggs.

baby chicks. It's important to understand that the eggs Miss Katie has been setting on are eggs from other hens since a setting hen stops laying eggs. And because Miss Katie seems to be so determined, Mama B has decided to let Miss Katie try to hatch a good-size brood. Using her hand to gently lift the little hen from her nest, Mama B places six more eggs from other Bantam hens under Miss Katie so that now she is setting on eight eggs. Mama B gets excited when there is a possibility of baby chicks on Bluebird Hill. As always, she never seems to have enough chickens. The fun part of raising chickens is hatching baby chicks from the eggs of her hens. That's why Mama B is perfectly happy to give Miss Katie the opportunity to hatch her very own baby chicks.

What tells Mama B that Miss Katie is serious about nesting is that she remains on the same nest almost constantly. When she does fly off for brief periods, she struts around in the chicken yard, holding her wings out and clucking. This is the motherly sound she would make

Miss Katie prepares for motherhood.

to baby chicks if she had them. In this way, she is alerting all the chickens, and Mama B too, that she is ready to take on the responsibility of hatching eggs. In other words, she wants baby chicks.

Miss Katie will be devoting the next twenty-one days to setting on the eggs before the baby chicks hatch. She knows she can get off the nest, but just long enough to eat, drink, and take a little walk, then it's back to the job of setting. Mama B understands Miss Katie's determination because she wants baby chicks as much as the little hen does. *All right, Miss Katie, you do the hatching and we will both share in the enjoyment of the baby chicks.*

Five days into the setting, Mama B realizes that she has left a wooden nest egg among the real eggs in Miss Katie's nest. The wooden nest egg is a fake egg that is placed in a nest to remind a hen where she is to lay her egg. A hen will lay an egg in a nest that does not have a nest egg, but Mama B's mama and grandmother always left a nest egg in a nest and Mama B feels right doing it as well. In years past, Mama B's grandmother used a small gourd as a nest egg. But Mama B's nest eggs are store-bought wooden eggs.

Realizing she has left the nest egg under the little hen, Mama B moves it to a nearby nest. The next day Mama B goes into the chicken

house to check on Miss Katie and to her dismay, she finds that her little mother has abandoned the real eggs, moved over to the nearby nest, and is happily setting on the wooden egg.

Moral to the story: Do not count your chickens before they hatch. And the lesson for Mama B is to be careful about removing nest eggs, especially if a nest egg is under a setting hen. Mama B also realizes she is not too old and never will be too old to learn something new in the chicken house on Bluebird Hill.

The king and queen of Mama B's chicken house.

Mr. and Mrs. Whitehead

The two White-Crested Black Polish biddies that Mama B bought at Tylertown Farm Supply grew quickly and Mama B couldn't wait to pick names for them. If you are a resident of Mama B's chicken house, you have to have a name. In case you don't know, chickens do not come when called by name. Nevertheless, Mama B enjoys naming each one of her chickens. Since one of her new biddies was a rooster and the other a pullet, soon to be a hen, Mama B named them Mr. and Mrs. Whitehead. Mama B could see that they were king and queen of the chicken house. No doubt about it. And they seemed to think the same about each other.

Mr. Whitehead, holding his head high, would strut around to show off his headdress of white feathers as the other chickens turned to admire his plumage. To add to his dramatic coloration, the comb on his head and between his eyes was bright red and V-shaped. Finally, as if Mr. Whitehead wasn't gorgeous enough, he had long black tail feathers, called sickles, which fell gracefully down from his back. His bare, featherless, gray legs were accented by long, intimidating

He was truly a sight when his iridescent black feathers changed color as he paraded in the sun, never bothering to cast a glance with his gold-rimmed eyes at any hen but his beloved Mrs. Whitehead.

spurs. (However, as you know from an earlier story, Mama B always trims off the sharp part of her roosters' spurs to prevent injury to other roosters or to people.) He was truly a sight when his iridescent black feathers changed color as he paraded in the sun, never bothering to cast a glance with his gold-rimmed eyes at any hen but his beloved Mrs. Whitehead.

Mrs. Whitehead was about half the size of Mr. Whitehead but her feathers had the same coloration, though her eyes were round and black. Her black tail feathers were layered and stood up in the back. She was not as colorful as Mr. Whitehead because she did not have red on her face. When Mr. Whitehead was able to keep her quietly by his side, they made a beautiful pair.

Keeping Mrs. Whitehead still was indeed a challenge and, in spite of their great beauty, Mr. and Mrs. Whitehead behaved in ways that

Mr. Whitehead was smitten by Mrs. Whitehead alone.

caused Mama B serious concern. For example, when Mama B would enter the chicken yard, Mr. Whitehead would run up behind her, flap his wings, and try to attack her. Mama B, always one to think the best of her brood, thought Mr. Whitehead might have remembered that she took care of him when he was a baby chicken and that he was now behaving aggressively to regain her attention. But it didn't take Mama B long to decide that she might have to give him that attention

There's no denying that Mr. Whitehead stands out in a crowd.

he was craving—but with the stick he forced her to carry for protection. Fortunately, Mama B didn't have to resort to such action, as Mr. Whitehead needed only to see her wielding the stick a few times before realizing that Mama B meant business. Later, when Mr. Whitehead would see her with that stick, instead of attacking, he would walk away, turning his head and keeping his gold-rimmed eyes on her every second.

In spite of his newfound respect for Mama B and her stick, Mr. Whitehead continued to strut and prance around with his beak up in the air as if he were king of the chicken yard.

Mrs. Whitehead, regal though she was, found it necessary to behave in a manner that Mama B found utterly exasperating. That little hen just had to run everywhere she went and often bumped into other chickens without even clucking an excuse me.

Much as Mama B hated to admit it, Mr. and Mrs. Whitehead were not chickens with good chicken manners or much intelligence. Of course, chickens aren't known to possess great intellect, but most do have good instincts and a bit of common sense. But the beautiful Whiteheads, sadly, seemed to be lacking both.

In spite of her beauty, Mama B felt that Mrs. Whitehead was lacking in both manners and sense.

Mrs. Whitehead, for example, just couldn't seem to get the egg-laying thing. There she would be, in the nest and scratching the straw, settling in the perfect position to lay an egg. Then, after about fifteen minutes on the nest, she would get off, cackling and celebrating as if she had laid an egg—but never was there a single egg.

But it was not all love and romance in the life of Mr. Whitehead because he had his issues with Lili. Lili, whose odd name is explained in an earlier story, is a large white rooster who has the perfect crow.

One day Mama B decided to play a trick on Mrs. Whitehead just to see what her reaction would be. Mama B filled the nest with an abundance of eggs. Sure enough, Mrs. Whitehead, with great exuberance, jumped up in the nest and settled her tiny body over the eggs as best as she could, as if she were setting. When Mama B gently picked her up off the nest and put her on the ground, instead of getting right back on as any good mother hen would do, that strange little thing ran as fast as she could to the other side of the chicken yard. Sadly, she just never seemed to know what proper chicken behavior should be. Finally Mama B had to accept the fact that if she was nothing else, Mrs. Whitehead was at least a pretty chicken and indeed the apple of Mr. Whitehead's gold-rimmed eye.

But it was not all love and romance in the life of Mr. Whitehead because he had his issues with Lili. Lili, whose odd name is explained

Just as Mama B thought, Mrs. Whitehead was soon off the nest and running as far from her duties as possible.

in an earlier story, is a large white rooster who has the perfect crow. And it has to be said that poor Mr. Whitehead, with all his good looks and swagger, had but a squeaky crow. As winter approached, Lili and Mr. Whitehead began fighting. It was never anything serious but nonetheless, Mama B does not want her roosters to fight. A rooster feud can escalate to several attacks a day and cause serious injury, resulting in the roosters having to be put in different pens or chicken yards.

One morning Mama B noticed that Mr. Whitehead was missing most of the pretty feathers on top of his head, and she knew immediately that he and Lili had been at it again. She quickly moved both Mr. and Mrs. Whitehead to another chicken yard. Though Mama B didn't quite understand it, the private quarters seemed to settle Mrs. Whitehead down and keep her happily by Mr. Whitehead's side. Maybe she sensed he was not feeling well and she was doing all she could to care for him. Perhaps she felt that her nearness would have a soothing effect and help him heal.

As part of the private chicken quarters, Mama B and Papa Doc built a small chicken house in the corner of the chicken yard so that guests could have protection from the cold weather. But Mr. and Mrs. Whitehead preferred to roost snuggled up together, on a roost pole, in the open chicken yard without any protection. As Mama B said time and time again, these Polish chickens are just beautiful but they have no sense at all.

One bitterly cold night early in February, Mr. Whitehead, who was still missing his thick feathers from his encounter with Lili, suffered frostbite on his head. This sent the poor creature into a downward spiral that ultimately led to his passing away.

Sad as his loss was, Mama B could never quite grasp the degree to which neither Mr. or Mrs. Whitehead possessed even basic chicken yard survival sense. And speaking of the lovely Mrs. Whitehead, the regal old thing went on to live a long life as a companion to Lili, the big white rooster with the odd name and the perfect crow. Once she was placed back in the flock with the other Bluebird Hill chickens, she returned to her strange ways. She never stopped running and she never laid an egg. But she was always queen of the chicken yard, viewed by all just as she was seen in the round, gold-rimmed eyes of the late Mr. Whitehead. And Mama B supposed that was enough for her.

She never stopped running and she never laid an egg. But she was always queen of the chicken yard

In the end, you could say that the moral to this story is that if you want to be productive and successful, it takes more than good looks. But if you're satisfied with mere celebrity, good looks will do'ya just fine on Bluebird Hill where there are always chickens, chickens, and more chickens.

Mama B and Papa Doc's calendar girl

From Stray Dog to Calendar Girl in Nine Months

After several stops at pet shelters and looking on petfinder.com Mama B tries petfinder one more time and this is what catches her eye.

Ginny — Shetland Sheepdog Sheltie
Size: Small Age: Young Sex: Female
ID: 2569
Notes: Ginny is approximately a year and a half old. She is spayed and current on vaccinations. She is very sweet, very loving. Wonderful little girl. If you are interested in Ginny, please contact us.
The pet is up to date with routine shots. The pet is already house trained. The pet has been altered.

SOUTHERN PAWS RESCUE, VICKSBURG, MS

Mama B had no choice but to have her beloved and faithful companion, Bo, put down because of cancer. He was in a lot of pain and Mama B knew when it had to be done. She had done everything she could for him during the last six months of his illness. It was time. Bo could never be replaced. He had his own special place in the life and heart of Mama B.

The next two months of Mama B's life without Bo were miserable. She had had a dog as a companion for her entire sixty-eight years of life. Now she felt incomplete without one. When she read the above description, Mama B felt certain that Ginny was the one—a Shetland Sheepdog, like Bo but totally different from Bo in color, size, and gender.

Mama B had never adopted a full-grown dog. She had always started out with a puppy. But in the aftermath of hurricane Katrina, when she worked with the wonderful people at her neighborhood animal shelter who had rescued and cared for the many dogs orphaned by the storm, Mama B learned to think first about adopting an adult dog in need of a home.

Mama B immediately e-mailed Southern Paws and learned that Ginny had been picked up as a stray and turned in to Southern Pines

Animal Rescue in Hattiesburg, Mississippi, on January 15, 2008. She was informed that when Ginny arrived, the poor creature had mange on her body and ringworm on her tail and her coat was badly matted. The people at the shelter told Mama B that Ginny was traumatized and terrified, shy of contact with humans, preferring the security of her crate. She had been examined immediately by a veterinarian, spayed and groomed at the shelter. Ginny was transferred to Southern Paws Animal Rescue in Vicksburg, Mississippi, for additional treatment for her skin problems. She also received lots of tender loving care to try to regain her trust. All of this treatment and care was given before she was posted on Petfinder.com.

The next two months of Mama B's life without Bo were miserable. She had had a dog as a companion for her entire sixty-eight years of life. Now she felt incomplete without one.

GINNY'S DIARY
WRITTEN BY MAMA B OF BLUEBIRD HILL

February 22, 2008

My friend and I drove to Vicksburg on a gloomy morning excited to meet and adopt Ginny. We were greeted by her foster mom who brought Ginny into the room to meet us. Head down with no expression, Ginny was wearing a rope leash and was very shy. I gently put a clean new collar and leash on her and sat on the floor to be at eye level with her and talked to her quietly for a few minutes. I signed the adoption papers giving Ginny a new home and me a challenge that would turn out to be wonderfully rewarding.

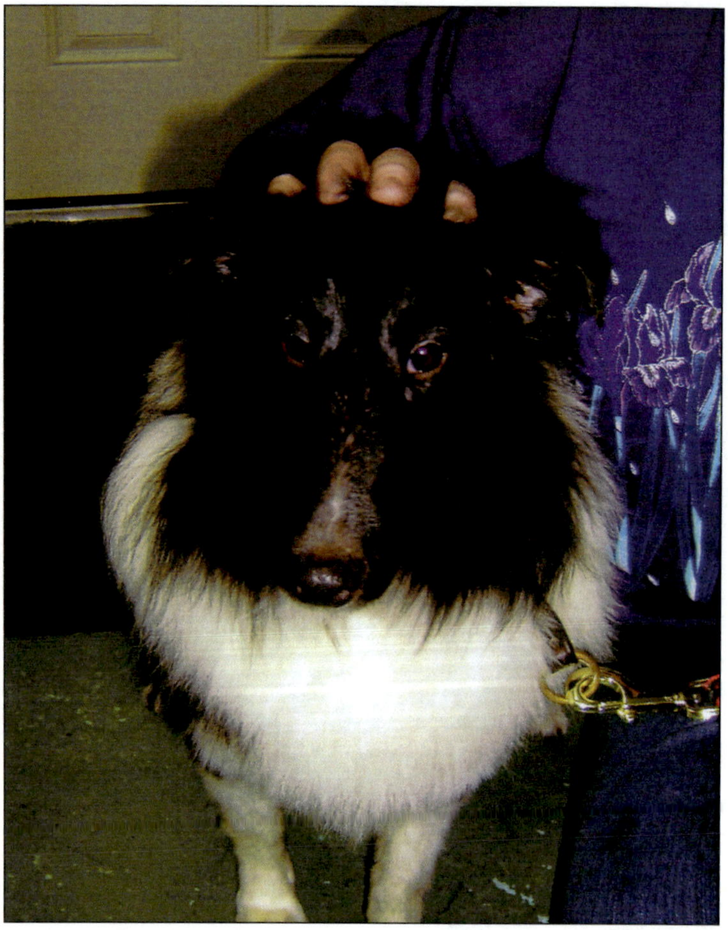

Ginny Jo still showing the traumas of life as a stray.

Trying to coax a sad and shy Ginny Jo to come a little closer.

Ginny cooperating but still not able to connect and fully trust.

The two-and-a-half-hour ride to her new home was uneventful for Ginny because she was in a crate, which was probably where she had spent most of her life before she was a stray. Once we were at home on Bluebird Hill, Ginny continued to prefer the security of her crate. If the door to the crate was open, she would pace in and out—not moving more than three feet from the crate. She nibbled her food and pushed it out of the bowl onto the floor and she drank very little water. Ginny showed no emotion and did not seem to know what to do with any kind of treat or toy. She only relieved herself once every twenty-four hours. Her ears were constantly down and back on her head, unlike most Shetland Sheepdogs whose ears are usually standing up in the alert mode. Ginny carried her tail between her legs like a Greyhound and the beautiful white fur on the tip on the tail, which is the hallmark of the breed, was gone due to ringworm.

February 23, 2008

We had our first photo shoot and Ginny actually did pretty good. She seemed quite taken with the smell of the narcissus blooming in the flower garden. I kept my foot firmly planted on the leash and although it was difficult to keep her still, I could tell that she was beginning to sense that someone loved her.

Ginny Jo beginning to trust and enjoy.

February 24, 2008

Progress day. I picked Ginny up and took her into the living room. I rubbed her tummy and played with her on the rug. While moving a toy back and forth, she started trying to catch it and yelped one time in excitement. The shrill bark actually startled her. It seemed that she did not know she could bark. She was learning about toys and the touch of someone who loved her.

I now close the door to the crate during the day and this makes her move around more in the house. She first ventured alone into the living room and then into our bedroom twenty-five feet away. She seems more alert and excited to be with us. At last she is showing some emotion.

Ginny and I took an afternoon walk—about a mile—using the leash. When I first tried the leash, Ginny went around me in circles and through my legs. She did not mind the collar but had no idea how to walk using a leash. All she wanted to do was sniff, sniff, sniff.

When we finished with our walk and I began to lead her inside, she folded all four legs down flat on the ground. She did not want to go on to the porch or inside the house. I did not know what this meant. She actually seemed to be afraid of the porch and the house.

February 25, 2008

This morning Ginny came into the living room and barked several times. She was responding to a large rubber ball I bought her as a welcome gift. She even made a *grrrrrr* sound at it. I do not know why she is afraid of a ball. Maybe she will enjoy it later. After lunch, Papa Doc, who was unaware of the ball incident, rolled a tennis ball near Ginny and she barked and ran as fast as she could to me in the kitchen. Since then she has stayed under my feet everywhere I go.

In spite of this, she did seem more at ease today. She is not pacing as much. I have kept her crate door closed and forced her to stay out and get used to us. This seems to be working. She is using Bo's big round plaid bed as her safety net now. Again, she gets on and off, goes only about three feet away, and then it's back on the bed. She is not as frightened. She is just uneasy.

We are getting on a potty schedule. She is eating her food in the morning without pushing it out of the bowl onto the floor. She wants to go for a walk early in the morning, about noon, and again around six in the evening. After that, forget it, she will not go. I'm just wasting my time. She likes to be in her crate by nine at night. I put a treat in and she goes in so quickly that she actually moves the crate. She does not make another sound until she hears me up around seven thirty in the morning. *Good girl!*

Ginny has made friends with Snow, our twelve-year-old cat who we found as a tiny stray kitten on the side of the road. Snow was Bo's good friend and he is excited to have another Sheltie in the house.

Ginny is ninety percent adjusted to us and she is a joy to have in our lives. Ever since she discovered she had a bark inside her body, she has definitely been a talker. She barks at everything—the phone

Ginny Jo and Snow the cat have a common bond.

ringing, the alarm clock, timer on stove, microwave buzzer, an acorn falling on the tin roof of the farmhouse. Even with all the progress, I knew it was going to be hard to get her ears up in the air and her tail carried like a proper Sheltie. I spent many hours the first three weeks with her in my lap, sitting on the floor, or in a chair. I rubbed her coat, talked very softly to her, and just let her know that I was her friend and did not intend to hurt her. All my effort paid off the first time I saw Ginny run on our farm without a leash—ears up, her white-tipped tail—now fully restored held high above her her body like a flag, her beautiful black-and-white coat, soft as silk,

Ginny Jo has made many friends on Bluebird Hill

blowing in the breeze—Ginny had found a home.

The name given to her at the shelter was Ginny in honor of Virginia "Ginny", manager of the animal shelter. Although she had clearly suffered as a stray, it was obvious to Virginia that with a lot of love and care this beautiful little creature could almost be a show dog. Virginia wanted to take Ginny home with her but she already had five pets and that was enough. Ginny was transferred to Southern Paws Animal Rescue. It is also a foster home for animals that need special care. (Most shelters do not have the time for one-on-one care.) I feel as if I was guided by my guardian angel to find Ginny and I am eternally thankful.

I changed her name to "Ginny Jo" in honor of my special friend, Jo McDivitt, who loves animals as much as Virginia and I do. With these two ladies as her namesake Ginny Jo has reason to believe she is very special.

When running on the farm she enjoys picking up sticks. Sometimes she drags one that is longer than she is. Could a stick have been her toy when she was living on the street? She loves to chase butterflies as they go from flower to flower. She tries to catch bugs and grasshoppers. Could insects have been her protein—a meal? There are so many unanswered questions about Ginny Jo's former life. No one ever contacted the animal shelter to see if she had been found. Is it possible that no one cared what happened to her or did some tragedy befall her owner?

Ginny Jo now wags her lush, white-tipped tail as she runs, and when her tail is at ease, the long white tip touches the floor. Her coat is soft as silk and easy to maintain. She wears a bright red collar with her name and phone number printed on the collar. Her jewelry is a St. Francis (protector of animals) medal dangling from a ring on her collar. And to insure her safety, she has a microchip. She has been to

Pet Smart for a Pet-A-Cure and is sporting bright red nails and a red polka dot bow in her hair today. She knows she looks good.

When we come back from a walk, Ginny Jo stops at the door to get her feet wiped and expects this whether they are wet from the dew or rain or completely dry. *Good girl! If only I could train Papa Doc!* She plays with her toys, enjoys her treats, and runs with Snow the cat. I'm sure they have lots to discuss since they were both homeless at one time.

October 5, 2008

I have entered Ginny Jo as a contestant in a Mississippi Spay and Neuter fundraiser. Her picture has been posted on their web site with several other dogs and cats. Friends and family of pets are asked to pay one dollar per vote for the best-looking pet. Based on the votes, thirteen will be chosen to be on the 2009 Mississippi Spay and Neuter Calendar—one for the cover and one for each month of the year.

November 7, 2008

Ginny Jo came in second place with 338 votes. She is honored to be the February calendar girl—the very month she was adopted and started her new life on Bluebird Hill. She has also been chosen to be media "spokesdog" to help raise money through calendar sales for the Mississippi Spay and Neuter program.

We have come a long way, Ginny Jo, and it was worth the effort. Mama B, Papa Doc, and all the animals on Bluebird Hill welcome you. You filled a big void and did it well.

Imagine, in only nine months Ginny Jo went from stray dog to calendar girl—WOW!

Sadly many dogs and cats have to be put down every year because shelters cannot care for all the animals brought in. There are many adult dogs living in shelters all over the country and each one needs a home. They can easily be found through petfinder.com or local animal shelters.

This is the photo that inspired Billie to write her books.

ABOUT THE AUTHOR

Author Billie Cole Remson grew up on a working farm in Collins, Mississippi where she acquired her love of nature. Billie and husband, Marcel, a retired dentist, divide their time between their home in Hattiesburg, Mississippi and their farm, Bluebird Hill, near Tylertown, Mississippi. Bluebird Hill is home to a multitude of Remson pets including Ginny Jo and Bear, their dogs, Snow the cat, a large flock of chickens, and a herd of cows and calves—all of whom serve as inspiration for her writings. Billie has authored four other books in what is known as the Bluebird Hill Series: *A Mississippi Spring on Bluebird Hill, A Mississippi Summer on Bluebird Hill, Katrina and the Unforgettable Mississippi Autumn on Bluebird Hill*, and *A Mississippi Winter on Bluebird Hill.*

WA